Technicolor Hans
and Other Events

Rebecca L. Davis

To order copies:
please email
dabeakdavis@yahoo.com
or click on
www.technicolorhans.com

Copyright © 2009 by Rebecca L. Davis

All poems and writings are original works written by Rebecca L. Davis.

All rights reserved. No part of this book may be reproduced in any manner whatsoever without written permission, except in the case of brief quotations embodied in critical articles and reviews.

Printed and bound in Canada

ArtBookbindery.com
Empowering Writers to Self-Publish™

ISBN 978-0-615-29806-1

Dedicated to:
(in no specific order)

Mom and Dad (Ann and Jim Rogers)
Phil Davis (husband)
My siblings and nieces and nephews (Jim, Marie, Deborah, Susan, Sarah, Jeffrey, Charlie, Michael, Kevin, William, Jason, Annie, Julia, Nicholaus, and Jacob)
Phil's entire family with Melissa and Kathy
Claudia Boosman
Father George Bertels
Father Al Rockers
Jane Curtin
Jan Ancker
Alice Smith
Operation Breakthrough (the Sisters and team) in Kansas City, MO
Neil Diamond and Rick Rubin
The Eagles
REO Speedwagon
Leann Morgan
John Schuler
Journey with Steve Perry
Paule Luce
Liz Cassidy
Fleetwood Mac all inclusive
Elton John
Diane Wubbenhorst
Lynne Howard
Kris Gronau
Susan Teters
Janet Taggart
Patrick Robichaud
Cynthia Lewman
Julia Turkin
Christopher Dineen
Cathy "cuzzy pooh" Wesner – and you know why we are smiling
Paul Biagi
Mark Dineen
William and Maggie Gelven

I woke up in the Louvre Museum
Renoir said, "is that a her or a him?"

That's an inside joke
And relevant at myself to poke.

Dali said, I don't care
I'll paint if she's Sonny or Cher.

Van Gogh leaned over on his olfactory nerve,
Saying, I have heard of her with a joyful verve.

Cezanne spun around; he was not even crude
I will certainly paint her in a tall, fully nude.

Degas was kind of in a mood of haughty.
He said, oh, no, she's over forty.

This place is fun, I must send my niece.
To meet the saint of paint, Henri Matisse.

Mountains of debt, bunch of greedy boobs.
We might need to borrow from Tony Shaloub.
The USA's a greedy monger.
We can't hang – any longer
Interest rates are lagging.
The economy is sagging.
Banks are not boulder teats.
From which we can eats.

No money in the guv-ment cash cow;
To save us somehow.

Hang on tight (to the)-
Political left or right.

Our big societal ill
    -   Is not a mole hill.

"They canvas the earth, these much do gooders"

They get dunked in paints –
By the laughter of Saints.

They work 24 x 7, eyes are bleary.
No rest for them, solidly weary.

They are picked up by their feet and brushed against the sands,
They are painted on the Nevadas and the Netherlands

They are amazing and only speak the Word
To comfort the tortured and the unheard.

I've seen them bury a sister
Then 8 hours later succor a listener.

Their heads dipped in paint to cover all flags unfurled;
God holds their feet and paints the world.

Because I believed,
A huge blessing received.

Rolling on, content with the "Wow."
I'm on the other side. Ha. What to do now?

Do I renig? It entered my head
And I'm lookin all around.
I can play till I'm dead.

I had popped through – happy as a clam
What? Another temptation.
Tow the line or feel the damnation.

What's the deal?
Drooping grin.
"Settle down, dork, to bow again."

A Day in the Life

We have hordes and masses of stupidity counselors standing by.
Driving, texting, and Twizzlers…don't ask why.

We have rows of editors standing and drooling;
These poems break rules and need retooling.

We have OCD counselors in a nice neat row.
They are anxious to help…don't ya know.

We have pizza dudes with dinner again;
Seen one often, I get looks of disdain.

Nutty ideas transform into action and feeling blue.
We have grief counselors standing by and they're crying too.

We have a medical team completely at the ready;
For the time beer before biking equaled unsteady.

We have ER personnel on whom to depend
As the dirt bike and rib are slow to mend.

We have Neil and the Eagles singin a song;
My name in Chinese is Sum ting wong.

Father Al says, "My Lord and my God."
Trying to hear it in the day's gloaming.

A couple of souls have been crushed in the sand;
But, it is not time for their Heavenly roaming.

Take our sediments of prayers to move them up,
First to kneel and then to stand.

This earth place beats us down.
Stack up our prayers, to make Ed, again grand.

Trina is here lying in wait
Please hear our fervent layers upon layer

She is here as part of the atoms.
Begging and believing You are: fine sediments of prayer.

Darin, my buddy,
You make my motherly instincts kick in
Your awful boo boo got more than your chin.

I'm not laughing at you –
Cause I've done some amazing street skids
At least you didn't gash both your eye lids.

This past Saturday I thought a dirt bike
Was just as light as a Trek
It fell on me and I said "heck."

Until your boo boos heal,
I will be your auntie and bring you booze.
But only until the scabs begin to ooze.

Then I'm outta here……………………………………….

Dear Santa

Here is my list and set of "Christmas topics" –
While I contemplate – the sunny Tropics

Throughout the year, Mr. Barry was extra nice
Please give him more, than just Old Spice.

Mr. Darin could be into crazy boxers,
Though he loves the shoes and the nutty sock-ers

I'm being bad and stealing a line from the clever Ms Howard
I couldn't think of my own, being such a coward.

Lynne said: please give Schuler some adult training wheels
And Wubben likes food – the kind that squeals.

Erik is a quiet man and we're not sure about the nookie,
He'll be fine with a milk and cookie.

Merry Christmas and Happy Holidays

"Let's go spread some Love – the Jeff and Hans show."

Hey Hans, let's go out that door
And home to lick them on the floor.

Let's go spread some cheer
You and a ball, me and a beer.

Hey, Jeff, Let's go spread some gooey hugs dripping from above
So many of your fans, bros and sisters need your Love.

Let's burn some calories and wear a smile
You gimme that Love for our next mile.

"oh, Becca, stop that cryin" – You go out that door and spread some sunshine
And "Bring them to Me"

"This one's for you"

Brother and Sisters – do you need a laugh?
Let's go ahead and do it on my behalf.

I'm not afraid to be a little wild.
Life is short to live only mild.

Remember the one from Hot August Night?
It's okay to talk about things that go bump in the night.

If you perform, "And the Grass won't pay no mind."
You will get dirt in your behinds.

That song makes me horny. And…..
It aint about roses, as they are too thorny.

The Evidence

My friends saw a party in the back of my car,
And I don't remember being the star.

They found control top hose, not on my feet.
And who put the beer in the car's back seat?

I have no recollection of the events from the past.
It must have been fun, but the memory don't last.

So little time and so many beers,
It's amazing I've lived this many years.

I can barely hang on
To this slippery round orb.
My fingers are dug into Africa
And I'm in self absorb.

Living in coo coo town
With my feet dangling in mid air
The planet is rotating
Stupid gravity isn't fair.

If I had my druthers
The sand of Africa would not hold the weight.
I could float to Pluto
To just sit there and wait.

You know, I know.
The other ball can't compare to here.
The Plan is intentional;
Pluto doesn't sell beer.

"Unemployed Blues"

Tennessee moon staring down on me
Momma says Jesus sittin up in a tree

Baby, baby, baby feelin down on my luck
Hockey gets to say you can take a flyin……puck

Lordy, Lordy, Lordy - this pity party fits a king
Honey honey honey hope I don't sell my ring

Tall lanky boy coming up for a hug
That feels better than a sip from a jug.

What we gonna do when we down on our luck
Gonna play hockey and take a flyin……puck.

Lordy, Lordy, Lordy, this pity party fits a king
Honey, honey, honey – there goes my ring.

"That guitar did not have a chance" he attacked it

That poor guitar did not have a chance;
Not even a sliver.
The Cherry Cherry opener caused the stadium to quiver.

I'm not kidding and you know what I'm talkin about.
You've seen the show; and did an orgasmic shout.

It is hilarious and people become spectacles
Getting front row to see some testicles.

I'm shaking and singing
My mom's ears are ringing

Oh baby – I can sing and dance – I have no choice
Gimme that guitar and sexy voice.

Who needs an organ in plain sight
When all you need is Hot August Night.

Uh-oh , there go the hips, and the pelvis.
Holly Holy – he woke up Elvis.

"Life in general and him in specific"

God turn this bitter dose into some form of power.
It has been a long slide down to this darkest hour.

Decisions of days and decades ago
Haunt us now looking up at the low.

Hate and discontent flow smoother than love.
How is that, when You are the Glove?

Tears streaming and landing on the dog's little head.
We stare up to You – please put us to bed.

"Come close to Me in your darkest hour.
I will give you sweet and no longer sour."

To Erik and Darin

How do I respect thee? Let me count the ways.
Your work increases merits and we all "gets" paid.

Most quiet need, by sun and candle-light
You make the "merit tunnel end" look very bright.

I respect thee to the depth and the breadth and the height
Your dedication creates customer delight.

How do I respect thee, let me count the ways,
Keep up the great work so I can count my raise!!

Certainly we all see the intentional take off on the poem
by Elizabeth Barrett Browning…..thank you, E.B.B.

Jack - did you have a Jill?
Do people say you are over the hill?

I don't know you, but Diny does
I am writing this just because.

I really think highly of the "Wubbenhoof"
She'll tell you why we say: woof, woof, woof!

I am sure you are cool, cause you know Diny
Debbie calls her Diny; and Debbie is finey.

It's your birthday and you dah man….
My husband is older, too, he needs a tan.

I hope you have good color and don't need some Sun,
But it's your birthday and this poem's fun!!!

Enjoy your day and give Woobey some grief,
Are you staring at this poem in disbelief?

Happy, happy day, Mr. Jack
You might get signing from Roberta Flack.

My boss has a name;
It is the Mr. Barry.

We have a history,
Even a bit scary.

He is from West Point
I like the beer joint.
He is reserved.
I am absurd.
He's totally brainy
I am quite zany.

He is button-down
I like to clown.

Yet, it took some time; something changed in the game
Enough thumps on the head and I'm not the same.

I still eat pizza and drink the beers
But Barry made me wise – beyond my years.

If you're ever in a bind – think "what would Barry do?"
And it's actually not – drink a Dew.

It's – learn from 'the Man' and truly listen.
He knows his stuff! It's not butt I'm kissin'

Jesus and the pair of bowls

Jesus, thus far, gives us two bowls, one of grief, death, and stress.
The second: 51% honey-dripping love on a constant hot egress.

This bowl feeds humans with heaps of heart.
The first bowl plainly tears us apart.

So far the bowls are not equal in weight.
What was intended? We have to wait.

Tired of rhyming for rhyming's sake.   Life and death comparable?
Jesus says so in the parables.

"To Kyle & Ronnie"
A symphony in the grass.
Hut hut hike!
The dance begins
And the partner is Spike.

Poetry in motion
Will get you a 10-yard flag.
Used to be 15,
Which was such a drag.

I'm cheering for you
You little Pop Warner.
Carry that loaf –
Around the corner.

Weekend dancing in the grass
What a pleasure!
Timing and inches
Must use a cup; but it's not to measure.

Hey, the dancing stopped!
Who coughed up the ball?
Grunt, sweat, bleed.
It must be Fall

There once was a rabbit
Who was Stuck in the habit

of mistaking a rock for an egg.

He'd find a pretty stone
Bite it like a bone

And realize the mistake he'd made.

He'd come upon a rock
And oh what a shock

To have eaten a morsel of jade.

All along the trails, both north and south
He'd find the jewels that hurt his mouth.

He just couldn't learn, and that was such a pity
He was destined for treats, that were oh so gritty.

Because this backward bunny had misadventures,
He's the only one with a set of dentures.

Happy Easter!!!

"a thirsty pancake – two trips to I-hop"

Somebody go get the syrup and pour it on three
I'm lonely down here with no butter on me

That's how many Coder eats.
He won't use a booster seat.

Pile up the answers and pile on the clues.
You've disappointed me with nothing I can use.

Today we are battered and beaten
And truly – more than half eaten.

Please coat me and heat me with tenderness.
I'm a soaking pancake, but really a complete mess.

Had i-hop with mike, jeff, and me
Sweet day that was – for all of us three.

A parched pancake waiting for our guy
Sure will be delicious when we don't need a why

Middle-aged woman Rapper (hip-hop style)

I likes to rocks and I like to rolls.
Shakin my booty, in my panty hose.

I can get down with the bitches and ho's
Swirling my head and my pointy nose.

Bump and grind at a teenage Rave
Can't go out, till the upper lip's shaved.

Gotta crank up, the car stereo
Drivin and jamming with my REO

Bustin a move for my nephs and nieces
They so embarrassed by my wools and fleeces.

This all I got, the rhymes all done.
Better put the hair, back in a bun.

"I do not like broccoli. And I haven't liked it since I was a little kid and my mother made me eat it. I am President of the United Sates, and I'm not going to eat any more broccoli."   President George Bush, Senior

I do not like broccoli Sam I am
I choke on broccoli; I am Cynthia. She said she is
That veggie in the wrong pipe put her in a tiz.

I do not like green peas and Spam
President Bush does not like broccoli said He.
Cynthia and Rebecca like Broccoli said We.

This is a weak poem, but it gets to the point.
Do not eat that veggie when you also inhale.
You will cough and snort, then switch to Kale.

All I have to do is Love God and stay on the road
5:29 pm

All I have to do is wake up, love God, and stay on the road
6:30 am

All I have to do is multi-task, Love God, and stay in the cube.

All I have to do is eat lunch, love God, and stay in the cube

All I do is sit atop a perch, Listen for God, and never move.
All I do is sit in this chair, Listen for God, and maybe move.

All I have to do is love God.   Monday.
Tuesday's agenda is set.

Holy nights are constant.
In the desert and
In the plains, blooming
Little pretties Reign.

Penitent hearts are longing.
Constantly straining and leaning;
Toward the One who leads them
With a very tinkling Rein.

"Waxing Poetically – I'll never go hungry"

One day the office was way too loud
I put soft, pink ear plugs in, to silence the crowd

Along came Cynthia with her good eye for funnies
To her, the plugs looked like pinkish, and golden gummies

She said something to me, but I couldn't hear well
My pink –   gummy –looking plugs had already swelled.

The plugs work super and I'm feelin good
And Gummies work as plugs as well as food.

My friend ordered pork,
Too big for her fork.

My friend ordered meat,
The size of pig's feet.

You know, I'm talkin' about…..
My friend ordered snout!!!

We saw the food. It made us say Woof!
That's the story of "our" Wubbenhoof.

"Later that night………."

She was proud of the nuggets and wanted to gloat,
But she ate 2 hooves and began to bloat.

The morsels were huge and I'm not being trite.
Later She was green and didn't feel right.

The world changed that day and we are not sure why.
All we know: is we laugh till we cry.

We'll continue to laugh and sometimes we howls.
But there is not envy, for the Wubbenhoof's bowels.

Spinal cords and brain stems

Atop the Eye of London, one sees some rain and sun tents throughout the year.
All the gray spinal cords and brain stems walking around have on some psychedelic gear.

Look at what those brains and spinal cords are wearing today
Dark casings, white pasty cases, yellow, red, leopard stripe; it's free - no have to pay.

Spinal cord brains have a lot of cushion from where I sat.
I have heard that covering is called extra fat.

Some cords are carrying beer and pizza. I like the ones who drum.
They are my new friends. Wonder where they stem from.

I'm wearing an outfit of some muscle and some cellulite under the ass.
There is a gal over there with colorful inkings on her underpass.

In the nursing home there is a pretty plain stem coughing up phlegm.
Put on some glasses. It's a rose on that stem.

I need a sexy glue-on mole

I've gone and done it…
I squeezed a zit.

It is the size of a dime
And it caused me to rhyme.

I thought it would just pop;
But I just couldn't stop.

That incessant pinching
And the "site is now inching"

I have now created a sore –
Must drive straight to the store

Where once there was skin – I have a red hole
Please, where can I get, a glue-on mole?

Oh baby I love to dance
Even though it is quite scary

Let's clone the voice
Which is Steve Perry

Oh baby I love to rock with REO
And Cronin who dances smoothe as a worm.

Let's keep them forever
And freeze his sperm.

O baby I love to move as a Diamond fan
Even before Rubin, Neil was the Man!

Gimme that Crunchy Granola Suite
I hear Neil has big feet…….

Wink wink

"Three for the money, go cat go"

Larry went jogging down the country road
He found a shiny dime
Just past the flattened toad.

Charlie Gelven had the Curly hair.
With Margie,   Momma and Pappa
Ended up with quite the pair.

I don't know how is it so.
How'd that dime get there?
Only know: I just want Moe.

Do you recognize this butt?

Twas the day before Wednesday and all through the lot,
Not a car was moving just Ron in a trot.

His truck was busted and he was getting pissed
He rented a new one, so he cussed and he hissed.

The cold had formed a piece of black glass
Ron strode on it and busted his ass.

Now his arse is the color of black and the blue;
Oh, Ron Helmer, it sucks to be you!

DC - Hammer is Darin (Instead of MC Hammer)

A hip, a hop, Ron got no Bop!
A hop, a hop, DC can't stop.

DC be jamming
And Ron aint hammin

Ron, listen to the man, a real soothsayer….
You need an ipod to be a real Player.

This is one of the *universal prayers to St. Jude; first published???*

Prayer to St. Jude
Most holy apostle, St. Jude, faithful servant and friend of Jesus, the Church honors and invokes you universally, as the patron of hopeless cases, of things almost despaired of. Pray for me, I am so helpless and alone. Make use I implore you, of that particular privilege given to you, to bring visible and speedy help where help is almost despaired of. Come to my assistance in this great need that I may receive the consolation and help of heaven in all my necessities, tribulations, and sufferings, particularly (*here make your request*) and that I may praise God with you and all the elect forever. I promise, O blessed St. Jude, to be ever mindful of this great favor, to always honor you as my special and powerful patron, and to gratefully encourage devotion to you. Amen.

- Author Unknown